GROWING MUSHROOM HANDBOOK

The Definitive Guide to Growing Mushrooms

AMBER MORRIS

Table of Contents

CHAPTER 1

The Definitive Guide to Growing Mushrooms

It's easier than you think to learn how to grow mushrooms.

Regardless of whether you plan to grow mushrooms as a hobby or a business, much of the same information can be applied to both.

As children, many of us saw our parents picking ripe vegetables from the garden, but it's still unusual to see people growing mushrooms at home.

If you've never grown mushrooms before, the idea of doing so can seem esoteric and complicated.

But don't be afraid of the idea, either. Grow your own mushrooms like any other fruit or vegetable once you learn the basics.

This article will teach you everything you need to know about growing mushrooms, from their life cycle to the best varieties to use.

The glossary at the end of the article can help you if you get stuck on any of the terms used in this piece.

Check out our YouTube video for the simplest way to grow your own mushrooms at home if you prefer to learn through videos:

How to Grow Mushrooms on a Small Farm or in Your Own Backyard

Mushrooms can be a great way to broaden your home or small-scale farm's range of crops.

For hundreds of years, people have been cultivating mushrooms in cramped quarters.

There are no limits to the types of environments in which mushrooms can be grown, even in terms of size.

Mushrooms can be grown both indoors and outdoors, whether in a repurposed basement or alongside your vegetable garden.

If you've always wanted to try your hand at mushroom cultivation, there's no better time than now to get started!

You don't need a lot of space to start growing your own mushrooms, even if you live in an apartment.

In contrast to conventional crops, there is no need to deal with the mess of a muddy soil. So, they're ideal for growing in a container indoors.

Our low-tech Oyster mushroom farm offers a glimpse into what a small-scale operation looks like:

Mushroom cultivation closely resembles the natural cycle of mushroom life. Changes have been made to improve yield and other aspects.

Mushroom Spawn

Obtaining spores or spawn is the first step in mushroom cultivation. Spors are well-known, but what exactly is spawn?

Any substance on which mycelium has already begun to grow can be used to expedite the mushroom-growing procedure.

Prepare a mushroom substrate with spawn or spores. Mycelium can grow on any substance that provides a suitable substrate.

It is common to refer to mushrooms as the "fruits" of the mycelium, as they are the primary food source for the fungi.

CHAPTER 2

Stage 2: Mushroom Substrate Inoculation

Inoculation is the next step.

Mushroom spawn or spores should be introduced to the substrate at this point (also known as a growing medium).

In order to prevent mold or other fungi from competing with your desired mushroom species, it's common practice to perform this step under sterile conditions.

Incubation is the 3 stage of the process.

Incubation is the next step after your substrate has been inoculated. This can take anywhere from a few weeks to a few months, depending on how long you keep your substrate in a warm, dark place.

At the end of this period, your mycelium will have completely colonized your substrate, leaving you with a white mat of mycelium around the perimeter of it.

Mushroom Fruiting at Stage 4

After the incubation period has ended, your substrate should be placed in fruiting conditions.

Cutting open the bag in which your substrate was stored to allow them to breathe in fresh air is the most common method. At this point, the substrate is misted with water throughout the day in order to maintain its moisture.

Pinheads (primordia) will begin to form on your substrate after a few days. Mushrooms of this size will eventually grow out of these.

Stage 5: Harvesting and Subsequent Harvests

You'll need to consider the type of mushroom you're cultivating when determining the best time to harvest them.

Mushrooms can be easily removed by simply gently removing the mushroom caps from their substrates.

Mushrooms can be harvested and replanted multiple times if harvested correctly. Whenever a new crop of mushrooms appears, it is said to be in a flush.

Eventually, your mushrooms will stop producing if your substrate is depleted of all of its energy.

Your initial mycelium will eventually succumb to senescence as you continue to use it to inoculate new batches of substrates.

All living things go through this deterioration as they get older. As a mushroom ages, it's basically in the same way as a human aging.

The mycelium loses its ability to grow and divide as a result of a lack of nutrients. When your mycelium begins to deteriorate, you'll need to get new spawn or spores and start over.

The Life Cycle of a Mushroom Farm

It's critical to understand the mushroom's life cycle.

You'll need this information if you want to grow mushrooms at home.

Typically, when people think of mushrooms, they only think of the visible stem and cap. Few people are aware of the extensive processes involved in cultivating mushrooms.

This includes a complex network of mycelium that is often much larger than the mushrooms you can see on the surface of a mushroom.

The root system of a plant resembles a network of cells called mycelium. But in reality, mycelium is more like the plant itself, while mushrooms are merely the fruit of that plant.

CHAPTER 3

Outside of the Shelter of Civilization

At the same tlme, the life cycle of a mushroom ends and begins simultaneously in nature.

When a mature mushroom releases its spores, the process begins. There are fungi seeds like there are for plants, and there are spores like there are for mushrooms.

When spores fall to the ground, they mix with other kinds of spores that are already in the area. As a result, the mycelium begins to grow.

A mycelium colony can consist of a single organism or a collection of individual organisms.

Pinheads will begin to form after the mycelium has had time to mature. These bumps will grow into mushrooms in the future.

Primordia, on the other hand, are an earlier stage that resembles tiny baby mushrooms.

When the mushrooms mature, they produce their own spores, and the cycle repeats itself over and over again.

Most Popular Mushrooms for Gardening

There are a wide variety of mushrooms to choose from, as well as a variety of ways to grow your own edible mushrooms.

In contrast to foraging for mushrooms in the wild, growing your own ensures that you won't accidentally prepare a poisonous specimen.

It is possible, but only if you obtain your progeny from reputable sources.

Among the most popular mushrooms to cultivate are the following:

- Mushrooms in the Shell

Beginners are most likely to grow these mushrooms. Although oyster mushrooms are less common in Western cuisine than button mushrooms, they are a staple in many Asian cuisines.

They have a look that you may have never seen before in a

mushroom. Due to the fact that they typically grow on the side of trees, they have a large flat cap with very little or no stem.

- Button / Cremini / Portobello Mushrooms /

Almost certainly, this is the only mushroom you've ever had the pleasure of eating.

All of these mushrooms are members of the same genus. Just how long they're allowed to grow before harvesting is the only difference between them.

Button mushrooms are the earliest stage of these mushrooms' development.

Cremini is the term used to describe them when they're a little older and have developed a brown color.

Eventually, they mature into a portobello mushroom. Aside from slicing or grilling them, they're also popular in soups and stews. Tougher and meatier in texture, they are more flavorful.

- Mushrooms with Shiitake Caps

Like portobellos, shiitake mushrooms are earthy in flavor and have a similar texture.

It's not only delicious, but it also has numerous health benefits, including compounds that can lower cholesterol.

Shiitake mushrooms are typically sold dried in supermarkets. If you can get your hands on some, it's a real treat.

- Enoki, number four

The long, thin stems of enoki mushrooms give them their diminutive size. They form dense clusters as they spread out. Because of their small caps, they would resemble strands of pasta more than anything else!

Because enoki are so small, minimal space is needed to grow them. Grown in jars is the most common way to cultivate them.

- Aside from being delicious, maitake mushrooms also have a wide range of nutritional and health Abenefits to offer.

Despite its common name, "hen of the woods," this mushroom is nothing to be confused with.

Because it looks like a hen's feathers and doesn't taste like one, it has been given this name.

The taste of maitake is very distinct, and we recommend sampling some before putting in the effort to cultivate it!

What You Need To Know About Growing Mushrooms

There are specific growing requirements for each type of mushroom.

Hardwood sawdust or wood can be used to grow shiitake mushrooms. Manure compost is essential for growing white button mushrooms and portobellos.

Straw, sawdust, coco coir, cardboard, and even coffee grounds are all good substrates for oyster mushrooms.

Indoor Mushroom Farming at Your House

Several methods exist for cultivating mushrooms in the comfort of your own home. It's a simple and fast way to grow your own food.

Packaged Mushrooms

Mushroom kits are a good investment if you're just getting started.

As soon as you receive a mushroom kit, you'll be able to begin cultivating the mushrooms right away.

Open the box, cut a hole in the bag, and spray or mist water on your gear every day is all that's required.

The little mushrooms will begin to appear about a week later. It should take two weeks for them to be ready to be harvested and savored.

Getting started with a kit is a great way to learn about mushrooms and the life cycle of a fungus.

You can avoid mold and contamination by skipping the more difficult parts of the mushroom growing process.

THE END